BRITAIN IN OLD P … HS

ILFRACOMBE

LOIS LAMPLUGH

ALAN SUTTON PUBLISHING LIMITED

Alan Sutton Publishing Limited
Phoenix Mill · Far Thrupp · Stroud
Gloucestershire · GL5 2BU

First published 1996

Cover photographs:
front: building of the new sea wall in progress in 1911; *back:* Ilfracombe harbour in the early twentieth century.

British Library Cataloguing in Publication Data
A catalogue record for this book is available from the British Library.

ISBN 0-7509-1141-7

Typeset in 10/12 Perpetua.
Typesetting and origination by
Alan Sutton Publishing Limited.
Printed in Great Britain by
Ebenezer Baylis, Worcester

CONTENTS

INTRODUCTION

Ilfracombe is commanded on its eastern side by the great head of Hillsborough, 450 ft above the sea. The accidental discovery of a Bronze Age tomb on the slopes of this hill indicated that people of that period may have settled in the area. The existence of an Iron Age fort around the crest of the hill is evidence that some Celts made their homes overlooking the sheltered cove that would become Ilfracombe harbour.

In the centuries after the withdrawal of the Roman legions from Britain, Saxons began to make their way westwards into Devon. By the last quarter of the seventh century, some may have begun to settle in the north of the county. Not until the Domesday survey was taken, however, do we have a name approximating to Ilfracombe: Alfreincoma, or the combe of the sons of Alfred – not the king of that name, but some unknown minor landowner. His eleventh-century successor was called Ailmar or Elmer; he paid geld, or tax, on one hide of land, usually taken as equalling 120 acres. Like almost all Saxons he was dispossessed, and the manor of Ilfracombe was handed over to the new Sheriff of Devon, Baldwin de Brionne. During the next few centuries, descendants of a Norman knight called Champernowne, from Chambernon in Normandy, were the foremost family in Ilfracombe. They held the patronage of the living, and one or two of them became its incumbents. It is possible that a small Saxon timber church had been built on the hill where today's parish church of the Holy Trinity stands, and also that the Normans built a defensive tower there which was incorporated into the later stone church. This had come into being by the thirteenth century, at the latest; the first parson whose name survives is Oliver de Tracy, instituted in 1263.

Four chapels were dependent on the church. Three were outside Ilfracombe itself, but the fourth was the little chapel of St Nicholas on Lantern Hill, above the harbour. This appears by name for the first time in 1416, but it is thought to have been built at least a hundred years earlier. It doubled as a tiny lighthouse; a beacon may have been lit on the hill in winter nights even before the chapel was built.

From the parish church to Lantern Hill is almost a mile. The space between them was filled in very slowly. In the early seventeenth century Ilfracombe consisted of 'one street lying scatteringly'. If by then most people were earning their living from the sea – rather than from the land, as in Saxon times – the area around the harbour was probably the most populous.

According to tradition, the harbour acquired a pier at some time in the fourteenth century. A commemorative tablet reads: 'This extensive Pier, built some Ages since by the Munificence of the Bourchiers, Barons of Fitzwarine, Earls of Bath and Vice Admirals of this Place, was in the year 1760 partly rebuilt, lengthened and enlarged by Sir Bourchier Wrey, Baronet, the present Lord and Inheritor of this Pier and Manor.'

For centuries Ilfracombe had been a port of embarkation for troops bound for Ireland. As early as 1208, King John ordered ships and men to gather there to carry soldiers across the Irish Channel, and later in the century Henry III directed a fleet to assemble for the same purpose. In the fourteenth century the port was called on several times to contribute ships and sailors for warlike expeditions. During the reign of Elizabeth I quite large drafts of soldiers – up to 800 at a time – were sent to Ilfracombe by way of Barnstaple to take ship as reinforcements for the Irish wars. In Napoleonic times English shipowners were required to supply ships in proportion to the trade of their ports; in 1795 no fewer than forty-nine were demanded from Ilfracombe. Two local families, the Bowens and the Downs, produced officers who served in Nelson's navy. One of them, Captain Richard Bowen, was killed during the ill-fated attack on Santa Cruz at which Nelson lost his right arm. Nelson said of Captain Bowen that 'a more enterprising, able and gallant officer does not grace His Majesty's naval service'.

Just once, in August 1644, Ilfracombe was the site of a battle. During the Civil War it was on the side of Parliament, and was attacked by a Royalist commander. He is said to have set fire to twenty-seven houses, but to have been beaten out by the townsmen, losing some of his men: the burial register records the names of ten men and one woman 'slain in the fight on the 20th day'. The name Bloody Meadow commemorated the event for centuries.

Shipbuilding may have been carried on in the harbour from the early Middle Ages. It is recorded that a partly built galley found on Lundy in 1242, and confiscated from its piratical owner, was taken to Ilfracombe for completion. Many of the small coasting vessels that traded from the port were probably built there, but the first known name is that of the brigantine *Edward*, of 60 tons, built in 1735. During the next hundred years or so dozens of little ships – brigantines, schooners, sloops and skiffs – were launched into the harbour. The biggest, the *Diana*, of 200 tons, was completed in the 1780s.

Yet by the late eighteenth century the sea itself was beginning to appear as a possible source of income for coastal places. A Dr Russell was attracting increasing numbers of people to Brighton, having put forward a theory that seabathing, and even drinking seawater, was a remedy for all kinds of ills. Soon even those not in search of salty cures were appreciating the pleasures of the seaside. It is somewhat surprising to find that, as early as July 1771, the Exeter *Flying Post* was claiming that many people had been visiting Ilfracombe 'for years past' and benefiting from its 'salubrious air and waters'. In 1822 the town was said to have been 'much frequented' in recent years as a bathing place, and there were warm baths 'for the accommodation of invalids'. Eight years later there were 'three good inns' and eighteen lodging houses. By 1878 there were about 190 lodging houses.

The population rose from 1,838 in 1801 to 8,557 in 1901. In the 1860s a group of entrepreneurs resolved to make Ilfracombe 'the Brighton of the South West'. Their efforts, and those of other developers in the next forty years, ensured that the architecture of much of the town belongs to the late nineteenth century. Perhaps the most quintessential Victorian building, on a splendid site overlooking Wildersmouth beach and the Capstone, was the Ilfracombe Hotel, designed 'in the French Gothic style' by a London architect, and opened in 1867. Thirty years later, Queen Victoria's Golden Jubilee was celebrated by the building of an elegant glass and iron structure, on the south side of the Capstone, as a winter garden. It was 200 ft long and 35 ft wide. In 1925 the central section was destroyed to make way for the Victoria Pavilion Theatre. The east and west wings survived for another half-century, and were then replaced by characterless concrete-walled rectangles, one used as a bar, the other as a public room. Ilfracombe Hotel was demolished, despite protests and a three-day enquiry, in 1976.

The arrival of the railway in 1874 (it had reached Barnstaple twenty years earlier) ensured that more and more holiday-makers came by train. Many others came by sea. Peter and Alec Campbell moved to Bristol from the Clyde in the 1880s and set up in business as owners of paddle-steamers offering excursions around the coasts of the Bristol Channel, including trips to Lundy.

Between the wars the number of car-borne visitors increased, but it was not until after 1945 that the majority travelled by road. The Barnstaple to Ilfracombe railway line closed in October 1970, and the much-loved paddle-steamers ceased to run in 1980, although the *Waverley*, owned and operated by a preservation trust, continues to visit Ilfracombe, as well as South Wales ports and Lundy, in summer.

During the past fifty years Ilfracombe has enlarged rapidly, climbing the steep slopes of its north-facing hills. From many parts of the country newcomers arrive, some to retire, others to take over businesses of one sort or another. Others again prefer, it seems, to be unemployed in a pleasant seaside town rather than in industrial cities.

Although in the last twenty years a number of factories have been built on the outskirts, tourism is likely to remain Ilfracombe's main source of income for the foreseeable future. Its obvious practical advantage is that, having been a resort for so long, it can offer a wide range of accommodation. Exmoor and the whole of north Devon are within easy reach. Above all, it is situated on a magnificent stretch of coast – much of it protected by the National Trust – while Hillsborough, Lantern Hill, the Capstone, the seven-crested ridge of the Torrs and the Cairn provide an exceptional setting.

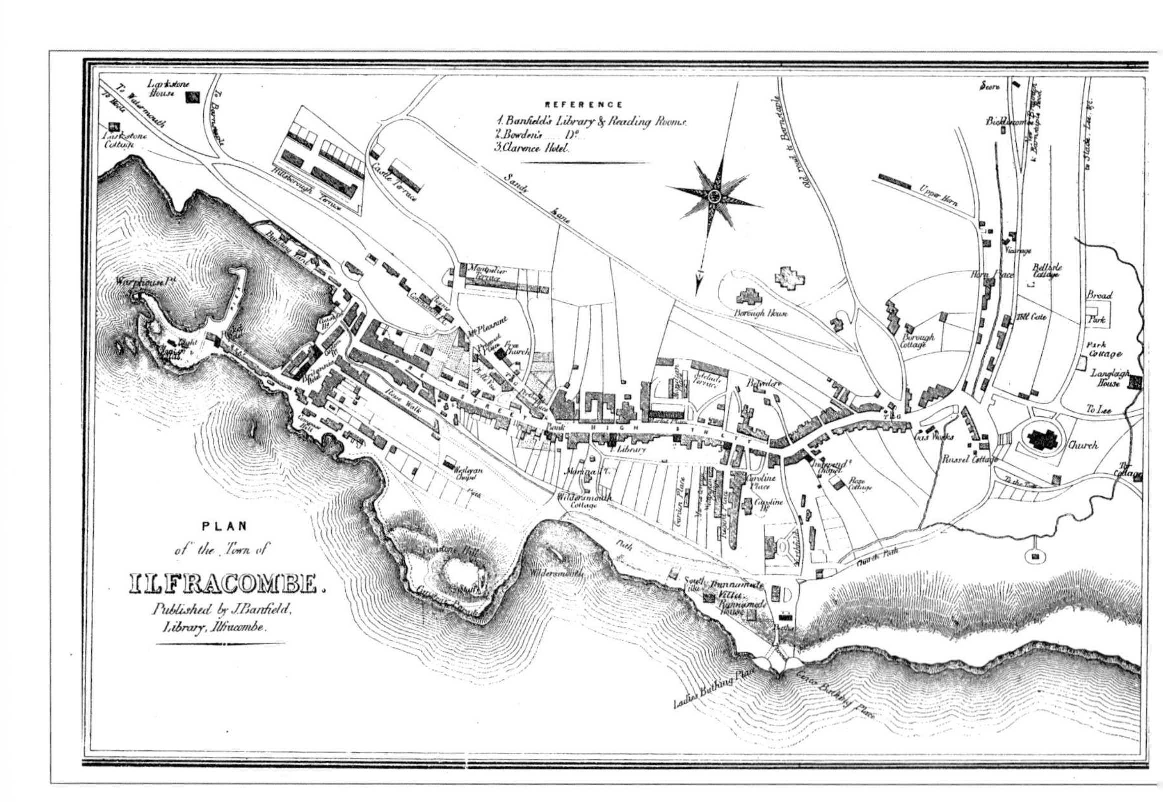

SECTION ONE

NINETEENTH-CENTURY ILFRACOMBE THROUGH ARTISTS' EYES

This panoramic view from the Cairn, looking east to the Capstone and a mountainous Hillsborough beyond, shows the whole of nineteenth-century Ilfracombe snugly contained below its hills, and the parish church of the Holy Trinity looking strangely isolated.

A closer look at the parish church.

Ilfracombe harbour around the middle of the nineteenth century, before the new pier was built in the early 1870s. The little ship approaching was probably a steam packet. As early as 1822 a steam packet called the *Duke of Lancaster*, sailing regularly from Bristol to Cork, began to call at Ilfracombe, and within the next twenty or thirty years others were also sailing to Swansea from Ilfracombe.

The Capstone slopes down to open meadows where sheep and cattle graze.

The artist stood on the eastern ridge of the Capstone to paint this view of Lantern Hill, houses around the harbour and Hillsborough. Here again a steam packet is coming in.

This view shows St Philip and St James' church, so would have been painted after 1857, when the church was completed after six years in the building.

The attractive little bathhouse 'in the Doric order', built by the Ilfracombe Sea Bathing Co. in 1836. The opening to the Tunnels beaches may be seen beside it. This was cut into what was then the open green hillside of the Runnacleave to provide access to two bathing beaches. In 1840 a writer recorded that 'the westward part is allotted to Gentlemen, while the eastward is by custom left to the Ladies and is carefully guarded against all intrusion.'

The Ladies' bathing beach at the Tunnels, provided with changing huts.

By the 1840s Ilfracombe was beginning to creep up its southern hills. The novelist George Eliot, staying in Ilfracombe in 1856, thought the new terraces were 'two factory-like lines of buildings'.

Another view from the Capstone, looking west across Ropery Meadow to the edge of the seven-crested ridge of the Torrs.

SECTION TWO

THE HARBOUR AREA

An apparently inferior copy of a painting of Ilfracombe harbour by Samuel Walters (1811–82). As Walters included the *London*, wrecked in 1796, he was depicting a partly imaginary scene.

A view from the south side of the harbour. Once again, an artist celebrates the presence of a steam packet to show Ilfracombe's connection with the modern world.

Ilfracombe had a tradition of shipbuilding going back to the thirteenth century. A map included in a guide book of about 1845 shows the shipbuilding yard on the south side of the harbour.

The harbour seen from Rapparee, *c.* 1860.

This large gathering on the pier below Lantern Hill looks as though it is waiting for some kind of entertainment, but were possibly members of a group outing waiting to embark on a paddle steamer.

Old houses in the area known as the Cove on the south side of the harbour. They were demolished before the building of a new sea wall in 1911. One was a blacksmith's shop.

Demolition of old buildings on the Cove.

Looking across the inner harbour as demolition work goes on.

Building of the new sea wall in progress in 1911.

Looking across to Larkstone beach, *c.* 1900. A paddle steamer waits at the pier.

The Revd Isaiah Siviter, vicar of Ilfracombe from 1925 to 1939, stands at the bow of the *Richard Crawley*, Ilfracombe's lifeboat from 1921 to 1936, to conduct a service. Fishing nets swathe the slopes of Lantern Hill.

A view of the Quay, 1925. The gentleman in the yachting cap is Mr Stephens, secretary of the Ilfracombe Lifeboat.

In this view of Ilfracombe from Hillsborough, the lifeboat house may be seen below Lantern Hill, where it still remains, although a new one is planned in Hierns Lane, with a new slipway to make launching of the lifeboat into the harbour quicker and easier.

SECTION THREE

AROUND THE TOWN

Like most towns in Britain, Ilfracombe ended the nineteenth century with a number of narrow back streets and clusters of very old houses that would be swept away within a decade or two. This photograph and several of those that follow show examples of this. Here is King Edward Square in 1907.

Water Lane, *c.* 1890.

A corner known as Parliament Square.

Another part of Water Lane.

Ropery Road before demolition in the 1920s. In the days of sail many coastal towns had their Rope Walks, Ropery Lanes or Ropery Roads.

Compass Hill, leading north from Broad Street.

Admiral Rodney Passage, *c*. 1890. The pub was named after Admiral Rodney (1718–92) who defeated the Spanish fleet off Cape St Vincent in 1780 and a French fleet off Dominica two years later. The pub's sign board is preserved in the Ilfracombe Museum.

Two views of the Golden Lion Inn. The picture above dates from *c.* 1885. In the picture below the man sitting down has been identified as Nicholas Lovering, and his companion as George Hopkins. The inn was demolished in 1893 when the Quay was widened, and rebuilt as the Pier Hotel.

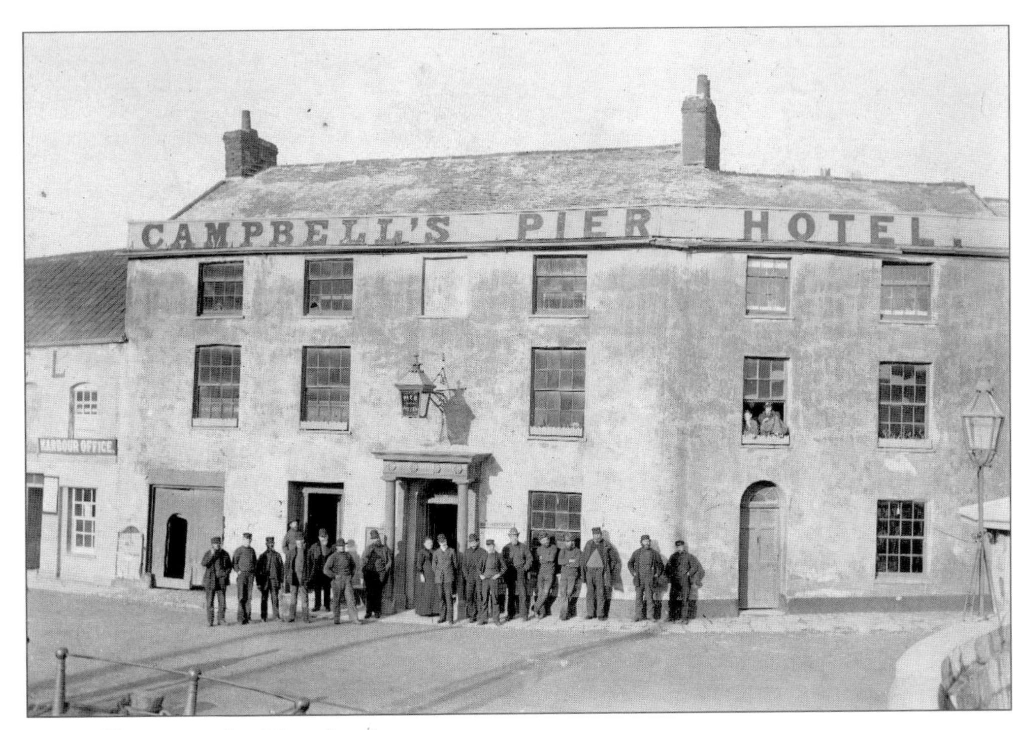

Campbell's Pier Hotel in Edwardian days.

Channings Crown Inn, rebuilt in 1895.

The Quay in the early twentieth century, showing the Newfoundland Hotel and the King's Arms, with the *Industry of Bridgwater* moored alongside.

This engraving of the eighteenth-century Britannia Hotel (later the Royal Britannia, after the future Edward VII stayed there for one night as a boy of fifteen in October 1856) shows that it was both a posting house and mail coach and steam packet office.

Coats's Boarding House and Dining Rooms in Broad Street, 1893. The adjoining building was then the Custom House.

Mrs Ann Popham had a shop in Broad Street at no. 7 in 1883. She later opened this boarding house on the corner of St James' Place and Broad Street.

St Philip and St James' church, completed in 1857.

This view of about 1880 from the Capstone shows Ilfracombe's southern hillside still only partly developed. The Wesleyan church in the foreground was later demolished.

From medieval times until the early twentieth century, it was necessary for towns and villages to have their own flour mills where locally grown corn was ground. Although the mill has gone, the street leading from Fore Street to the Promenade is still called Mill Head.

The Promenade from the Gilbert Hotel. By 1906 the Ilfracombe Urban District Council had bought Ropery Meadow for £2,203 for use as a recreation ground; paths had been laid out and seats fixed. In 1922 this developed into the Victoria Pleasure Grounds, with bowling and putting greens. The Ilfracombe Hotel, demolished in 1976, appears in the distance, with the Granville Hotel on high ground beyond.

This photograph seems to have been taken from the tower of St Philip and St James' church. Although similar to the previous picture, it shows the Victoria Pavilion theatre, opened in May 1925. The central section of the old Pavilion or Winter Garden was destroyed to accommodate it, though the east and west wings were allowed to remain a few decades longer, to be replaced eventually by two concrete-walled rectangles, one in use as a bar and the other as a public rest room where art exhibitions are sometimes held.

The Ilfracombe Hotel, opened in May 1867, was enlarged in 1871. An advertisement of 1895, aimed at Indian and Colonial visitors, announced that it had 250 apartments, handsome public rooms, ornamental grounds of 5 acres and eight lawn tennis courts.

A view of the delightful glass and iron Victoria Pavilion, not long before the destruction of its central section. It was opened in 1888 to celebrate Victoria's Golden Jubilee. Locally it was at first known simply as 'The Shelter', or sometimes as 'The Cucumber Frame'.

This all-male group of very respectable looking townspeople, including a Dr Stoneham, was photographed outside the east wing of the Victoria Pavilion in about 1890.

The interior of the Victoria Pavilion, with seats arranged as though for a concert – perhaps by one of the 'season bands' that played both in the Pavilion and at the nearby bandstand in summer.

People enjoying the shelter of the Victoria Pavilion, with its palms and climbing plants, around the turn of the century.

This fountain in what was still known as Ropery Meadow was set up in 1890 as a gift from a visitor, but removed, regrettably, during the conversion work in 1922.

The Parade, showing the bandstand and the west wing of the Victoria Pavilion, *c.* 1910.

Looking out over Wildersmouth beach from the Capstone, *c.* 1912.

In the late nineteenth and early twentieth centuries, 'Lifeboat Thursday' was celebrated on the first Thursday in September to raise funds. This crowd on Wildersmouth beach was watching the lifeboat offshore.

The couple in this not-very-saucy Edwardian photograph are on the North Parade of the Capstone, where shelters and many seats were provided for townspeople and visitors.

Two views of the Runnacleave Hotel, the second perhaps twenty years later than the first. The hotel was completed in the summer of 1891, and the adjoining Runnacleave Hall, which could seat between five and six hundred people, was opened on Whit Monday 1892 with a concert. A directory listed it as the Runnacleave Theatre and Opera House.

The High Street, looking west, with Sam Colwill's four-in-hand team of greys drawing the Lynton coach, *c.* 1905.

The High Street again, a year or two later, looking east. The raised bank on the south side of the street was removed after the Second World War.

John Myatt opened a bookshop at 41 High Street at some time between 1884 and 1897. By 1914 William Walton Myatt, presumably John's son, had moved to the corner of Northfield Road and the High Street. He sold maps and guides, London and provincial newspapers, playing cards, draughts and chess sets and much else. In 1935 Ilfracombe's new Gas Offices were built on the site.

The east end of the High Street: Fore Street on the left, Portland Street on the right.

Mr Cole's furniture shop, triumphantly rebuilt after Ilfracombe's 'Great Fire' of 1896.

Fore Street, *c.* 1900, when C. Rudall's sign announced that he was a Decorative House Painter, a Mr Comer ran a butcher's shop and visitors could stay at the Seaview Boarding House.

Church Street, *c.* 1910.

Another view of Church Street, when it had a pub called the Ring of Bells.

Horne Road, leading off Church Street, as it was in the early years of the twentieth century.

Holy Trinity parish church, before the days of motor traffic.

The War Memorial Gardens were opened by Lord Fortescue on Armistice Day, 1924.

An Edwardian family and their servants stand in the sun outside a house in Slade Road.

St Brannock's Park was developed in the 1880s. No. 14, Holloways, seen here, was built in 1890.

A typical example of late-Victorian Devon domestic architecture, showing the neo-Gothic influence of the period. This is the Gables, Belmont Road.

Tyrrell Cottage Hospital. In 1864 Mrs Anne Tyrrell provided two beds in a cottage in Horne Lane 'to see whether it would be a benefit to the poor'. Her initiative was so successful that in 1870 a purpose-built hospital was opened in Higher Horne.

An aerial view of Bicclescombe Park in the years between the wars.

Score Valley, as it was in about 1914.

The old road to the Cairn, which had become a public pleasure ground by 1906. It is now a nature reserve in the care of the Devon Wildlife Trust.

The Round House on the edge of the Cairn, said to have been built by a businessman determined to have views on all sides.

Torrs Walks, cut in the seaward slopes of the great ridge that protects Ilfracombe on its western side. As early as 1856 the novelist George Eliot was daunted to find that an admission charge of 3*d* was made at the entrance.

At the eastern end of the town, the open spaces of Hillsborough were protected from speculative builders in the 1890s, when the Ilfracombe Urban District Council took over from the old Board of Health.

The Southern Slope Gardens, with the Granville Hotel high on its hill, and the Ilfracombe Museum, housed in the old Ilfracombe Hotel's laundry building (it still bears the date 1885) half-hidden behind the tree on the right.

Chambercombe Woods in the early twentieth century.

Section Four

People

Sir Bourchier Palk Wrey with his second wife near the ancient Warphouse at the entrance to the harbour. (Warphouse Point was filled in when the new pier, made possible by a loan of £10,000 from Sir Bourchier, was built in the early 1870s.) He was a descendant of the Bourchiers, Barons Fitzwarine, who held the harbour manor of Ilfracombe for centuries. This photograph was probably taken at some time in the 1860s. Sir Bourchier died, aged ninety-one, in 1879.

In 1843 the opening of the Capstone Parade – cut largely to give work to local unemployed – was celebrated with a public tea, fireworks and two balls, one of them for tradesmen. This group was probably photographed towards the end of the nineteenth century.

Prebendary John Mill Chanter, vicar of Ilfracombe from 1836 to 1887, with his wife Charlotte outside the old vicarage, which was demolished in 1888. Charlotte Chanter was a sister of Charles Kingsley.

Elegantly dressed ladies and gentlemen enjoying the sea view on the north side of the Capstone. The church of St Philip and St James may be seen in the background. Style of dress may date this to the late 1860s.

Until well into the twentieth century, many country people travelled to their local towns by pony and trap. Here Dick Leewell and his wife are seen on their way to Ilfracombe market from Combe Martin.

The photographer captioned this 'The Boys of the Village', but they would seem to working on the railway – perhaps shortly before the London and South Western's line was continued from Barnstaple to Ilfracombe in 1874.

Mr Sollis, who was the guard on the first train to run to Ilfracombe in 1874.

Tom Colwill, son of the redoubtable Sam Colwill, took over as driver of the Ilfracombe to Lynton coach when his father retired, having worked as his assistant driver for some years. In August 1892, a reporter from the *Midland Times and Gazette* described Tom as a careful driver who evidently took great care of his horses: 'He calls them his "dears" and "darlings" and talks to them like rational beings.' Like his father, Tom had a fund of anecdotes with which he entertained his passengers.

One of the 'season bands' which played in the Victorian Pavilion or at the bandstands (the pier had its own bandstand) each summer.

Mr Bassett of Watermouth Castle with his hounds Duster, Monitor and Landlord.

Robert Martin, an ex-soldier who served for many years as Ilfracombe's mounted town crier. He died at Woolwich in 1922.

It might be thought that almost the whole population of '90s Ilfracombe had turned out to celebrate the wedding, in 1893, of the Duke and Duchess of York, who were to become King George V and Queen Mary.

In 1905 a William Kibble let apartments at 5 Capstone Crescent, but by 1910 he had converted houses opposite to the Moonta Hotel. Presumably the donkey riders were holiday-makers staying at the hotel.

A Rechabite gathering, 1896. Ilfracombe's Rechabite Central Hall was built in 1905 at a cost of £2,000.

This photograph, taken by F. Grattan Phillipse of the Royal Kingsley Studio, shows Ilfracombe National Boys' School (Holy Trinity) during the headmastership of Mr H.J. Macey.

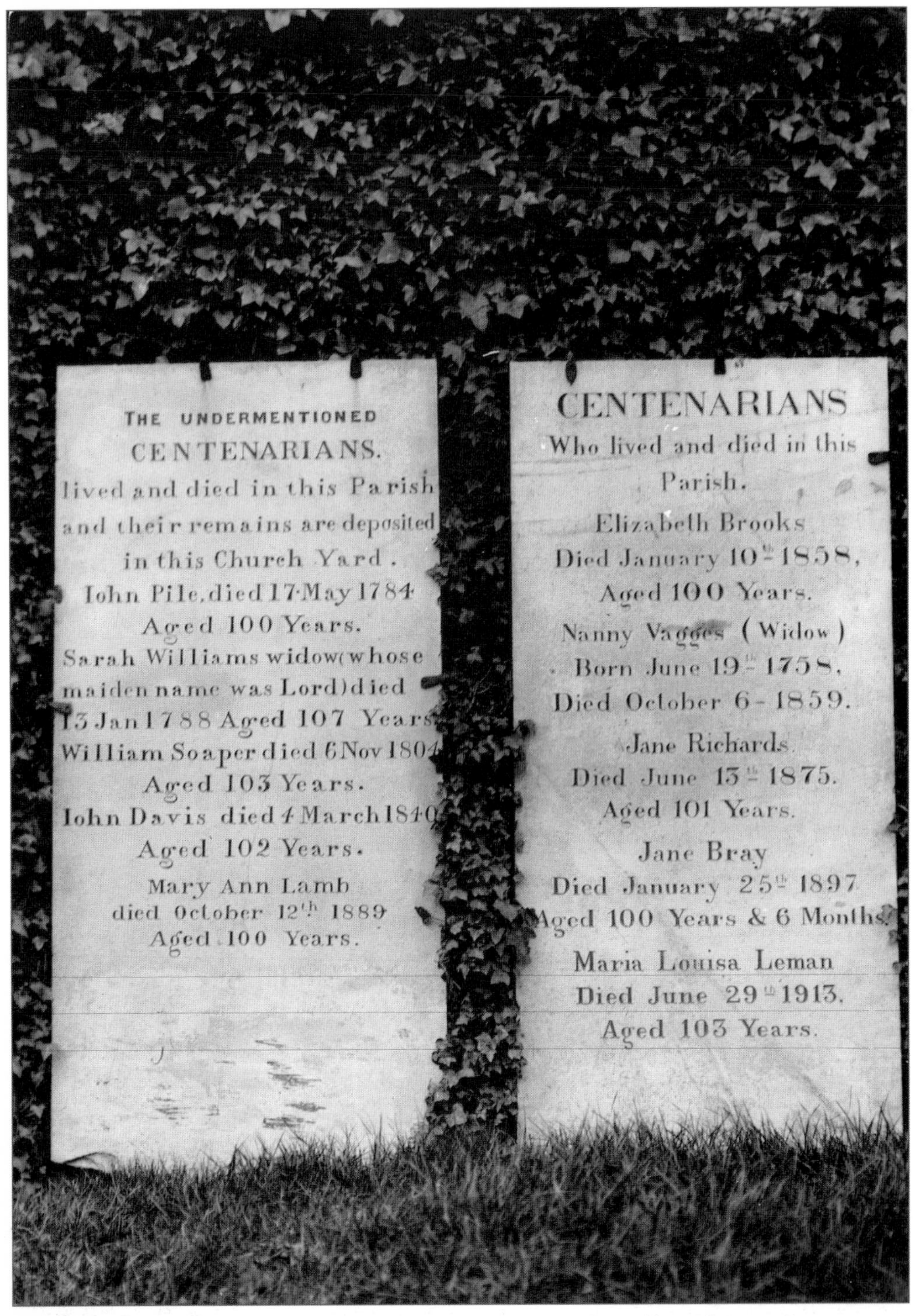

From the beginning of its life as a holiday resort and retirement place, Ilfracombe was always eager to stress its healthy climate. These two slate tablets, clamped to the outer wall of the parish church, record the names of three men and seven women who attained the age of a hundred or more between 1784 and 1913.

The last name on the centenarians' tablet is that of Miss Maria Louisa Leman, seen here, in August 1912, ten months before she died. She was one of the eight children of a solicitor in Clifton, Bristol, but spent half her life in Ilfracombe. A devoted churchgoer, she was said to have enjoyed 'splendid health' until shortly before her death. (The baby elephant apparently belonged to a visiting circus.)

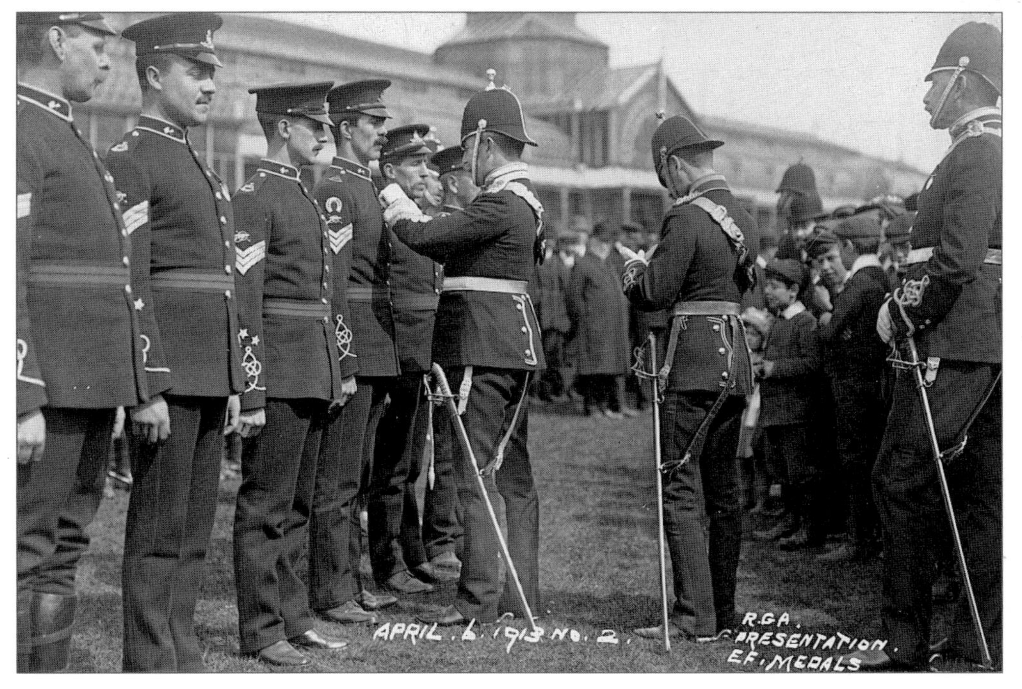

These soldiers receiving medals in April 1913 were Territorials, members of No. I Heavy Battery, Devonshire Royal Garrison Artillery, which had its headquarters at Ilfracombe. Probably some of these men were on active service in France within eighteen months of this ceremony.

A company of Ilfracombe Girl Guides, photographed in August 1915.

The seamen posing for the camera in the days before a wall was built along the Quay have been identified as W. Barbeary, S. Williams, S. Groves and W. Davy.

Territorials marching past the cab rank alongside the raised bank in the High Street, on their way to camp in April 1912.

This group of soldiers, posing with a framed picture of Ilfracombe's town arms, may have been involved in a First World War recruiting drive.

Children from the Infants' Department of the National School celebrating Empire Day with a Maypole Dance, 1906.

The apparent mildness of a March day in 1908 evidently drew this large group of women and children to sit in the sun outside the Victoria Pavilion.

Archdeacon Seymour of Barnstaple and Prebendary George Tugwell pose for the photographer outside Ilfracombe Vicarage on some special occasion, *c.* 1900. Mr Tugwell, a graduate of Oxford, was the author of a number of books. When the novelist George Eliot visited Ilfracombe in 1856, she and the writer with whom she lived, George Henry Lewes, sought out Tugwell, then a young curate, because they had read his book on sea anemones. He became the first incumbent of Lee, and died in 1910.

Men taking a rest from building the Scarlet Pimpernel garage, 1919. Scarlet Pimpernel charabancs ran trips to many places in Devon in the 1920s and 1930s.

The swimming baths built for the use of guests at the Ilfracombe Hotel became the town's Municipal Baths, and many swimming galas were held there. This one was in 1923.

Pupils and staff of Herefore House School, Torrs Park, July 1937. In 1878 a Mrs Maunder ran a 'seminary for young ladies' at Palmerston House, Torrs Park. Later her two unmarried daughters carried on what they called a 'ladies' school' at Herefore House. Miss Mary Jones (seen here in dark clothes) had taken over by 1919, with her sister, Miss Charlotte. At the beginning of the Second World War Mary retired and was succeeded by Miss Ethel Theak (sitting on her right). At that time the Collins sisters – Joan the film star and Jackie the novelist – were pupils.

A smart turn-out of young Baptists and their band.

'The King of Sherwood', a comic operetta by Thomas Hewitt, was presented in 1928 at what the *North Devon Journal* called the Victoria Pavilion Concert Hall by members and friends of the Wesley Guild, assisted by the Ilfracombe Amateur Orchestral Society. The *Journal* said that 'the chorus was most tuneful throughout, and the dresses highly effective'. At this time Ilfracombe was well provided with places for theatrical performances. In addition to the Victoria Pavilion there was the Runnacleave Hall, the Alexandra Hall and the Gaiety Theatre.

Each summer Ilfracombe holds a Victorian Week, with a number of events at which people dress in appropriate costume. In June 1992, the Museum staff posed for this photograph at the entrance to the Museum. Standing, left to right, front row: Colin James, Joy Slocombe (Curator), Jean Hardwicke. Back row: David Hunt, Reg Hodder, Sam Ley.

SECTION FIVE

SPECIAL EVENTS

In July 1874, having waited twenty years for the London and South Western Railway to continue its line from Barnstaple to Ilfracombe, the people of Ilfracombe rejoiced at the arrival of the first train at the station high to the west of the town. Streets were decorated with triumphal arches such as this one, bearing cheerful mottoes: 'Success to the Railway', 'Prosperity to the Town' and 'May the Rails of the New Line never Rust'. In October 1970, the line closed.

A procession passing the Runnacleave Hotel in Wilder Road during local celebrations of Queen Victoria's Diamond Jubilee, 1887.

It is surprising to find that Ilfracombe saw the ascent of a hot air balloon as early as 1894. The open space on which it was being inflated was later developed as Greenclose Road.

An inspection parade of Ilfracombe Volunteers on the pier, 1894.

The Devonshire Regiment, having marched from Barnstaple, on the Quay in 1895. They were bound for Newport in South Wales. They embarked on the paddle steamers *Westward Ho!* and *Cambria*.

The aftermath of Ilfracombe's Great Fire of 1896. It began in the furniture and ironmongery shop of William Cole, at the junction of Portland Street and Fore Street, leapt across the High Street and down the Arcade. More than thirty houses and shops were gutted, and the ruins went on smouldering for several days, but there was no loss of life. This area of the town was to see an almost equally destructive fire in September 1983, when the Arcade and the Candar Hotel burned down, and one man died.

The opening of Ilfracombe's new waterworks in July 1904 was performed by Lord Ebrington, Lord Lieutenant of Devon, and attended by many local notables, including the Devon-born general Sir Redvers Buller, whose relief of Ladysmith in February 1900 made him a national hero.

On a wet day in October 1911, members of what was described as the canteen party trot along the High Street. Although not in uniform, they may have been Territorials going to camp.

One evening in December 1910, a freak storm at high tide battered many places along the south coast of England. In Ilfracombe a furious westerly gale swept a great surge of water across Capstone Parade and Ropery Meadow (as it was still known), ripping up roadways and demolishing masonry. The sea wall at Cheyne Beach was broken in several places and the pier was damaged.

On a number of occasions Ilfracombe celebrated some special event with a display of what were referred to as 'Living Letters'. This one in 1910 marked the coronation of King George V and Queen Mary.

It seems that on 8 August 1914 most of the population of Ilfracombe attended a service conducted from the raised bank in the High Street by Prebendary H.M. Johnson, vicar of the parish from 1909 to 1938, as the local Territorials of the 1st Heavy Battery, Devonshire Royal Garrison Artillery, prepared to leave.

Led by the band, the column of Territorials marches down the High Street on their way to the station, on an evidently wet day in August 1914.

After the ending of the First World War the official Peace Day was celebrated on 19 July 1919. Once again, Ilfracombe paid its tribute in Living Letters.

A 'Children's Victory Tea' in St. Brannock's Park, Ilfracombe, in 1945. Many similar street parties were organized in other parts of the town, and military parades and a Thankgiving Service were held to celebrate VE Day.

SECTION SIX

TRANSPORT

Frank Knill, coachbuilder, outside his workshop. The vehicle on view has been identified as a barouche with the name 'Midge'.

Cabs lined up in Ilfracombe High Street during local celebrations of the wedding of the Duke and Duchess of York (later King George V and Queen Mary) in 1893. In north Devon it would be some thirty years before the horse-drawn cab began to be superseded by motorized vehicles.

For twenty years Sam Colwill, seen here on the box of the Ilfracombe to Lynton four-in-hand, drove a coach to connect the trains arriving at Barnstaple, until the line was extended to Ilfracombe in 1874. From then on, for 35 years or so, he ran a regular summer service to Lynton.

Sam Colwill's coach was named Benita, after Benita Odam, Lorna Doone's nurse in Blackmore's romance. Each morning it was said to sweep through the town 'with the guard blowing his horn occasionally to clear the road of the many carts that obstruct our narrow thoroughfares'. Here Sam, nearly eighty, stands at the horses' heads on a July day in 1906. His son Tom is on the box.

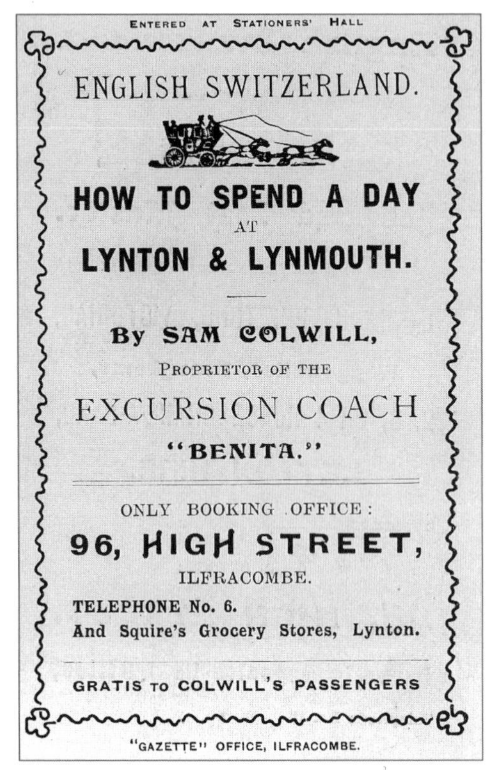

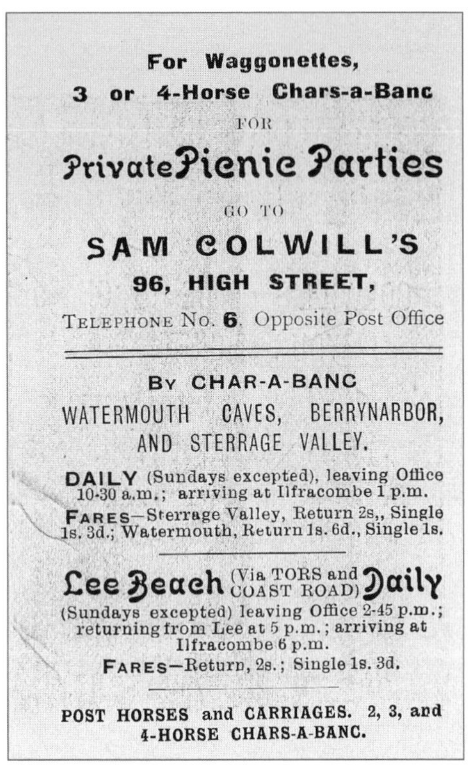

Sam Colwill published a small booklet which he handed out to passengers on his coach. As these advertisement pages show, he later ran charabanc tours to many nearby places, including Barnstaple. This song by two local men, Alan Hussell, an architect, and Will Coates, who as a young man worked at Mr Cole's furniture shop at which the 'Great Fire' began, shows the great popularity of 'Coachman Sam'. The words ran:

'I'll sing you a song of the olden days,
The coaching days, the golden days,
Of Coachman Sam and his team of greys
On the Lynton road in the morning;
Our Sam was happy, blithe and gay,
Happy he as the birds in May,
For with tale and song he beguiled the way
On the Lynton road in the morning.
Then sing Heigh Ho! for the olden days
The rollicking, galloping coaching days,
And sing Heigh Ho! for Sam and his greys
On the Lynton road in the morning.

Sam's team was the pride of the West Countrie,
That fair countrie, my dear countrie,
And never a grander drive there be
Than the Lynton road in the morning.
It winds along by the deep blue sea,
Past valley and rock, green meadow and tree,
The horn's merry notes rang cheerily
O'er the Lynton road in the morning.'

The cover of the sheet music for the song 'Coachman Sam.'

By 1897 Lake and Copp were advertising Copp's Coaching Trips. They had several named coaches. Their 'Defiance' ran daily to Lynton in competition with Colwill's 'Benita'; their 'Katerfelto' visited Watermouth, and their 'Dreadnought' ran to Woolacombe and Combe Martin and to Barnstaple on Fridays (market days). Mr Copp's coachhorn is preserved in the Ilfracombe Museum, as are the coachhorn and whip of Sam Colwill.

One of Copp's coaches with a full load of passengers outside the Royal Clarence Hotel in Ilfracombe High Street, August 1906.

As the song 'Coachman Sam' says, Sam Colwill almost always drove a team of greys. The steep hills on the 19 mile drive from Ilfracombe to Lynton made it necessary to change horses halfway. Evidently passengers were not expected to dismount while this was going on.

Ilfracombe station, when it was first opened in 1874.

The 'Devon Belle' leaving Ilfracombe. This Pullman express service only ran between Waterloo and Ilfracombe from 1947 to 1954. The proudly named Atlantic Coast Express, first introduced in 1926 and restored after the break caused by the Second World War, ran for the last time on 5 September 1964.

From this delightful little locomotive-shaped vehicle the enterprising owners sold fish and chips.

Every available coach in Ilfracombe must have come into service during the holiday months in the early years of the twentieth century. Passengers here are Lancashire mill workers, August 1911.

As early as 1816 a visitor to Ilfracombe observed that 'all wheel conveyance' was done by donkey chairs. In the 1890s a bylaw laid down that there was to be not more than one passenger in any donkey carriage. At the same time it is evident from this photograph that donkeys to ride were numerous – and it may be noted that, even on donkeys, Edwardian ladies rode side-saddle.

The first motor car in Ilfracombe was owned by Mr William Gant, seen here with his son Jack and daughters Florence and Evelyn. Mr Gant owned a coffee house on the Quay in the late nineteenth century. By 1902 this was referred to as refreshment rooms. He also owned a fish and chip shop in Fore Street, and later was a boarding house proprietor.

Mr Woodward, senior, of Slade Laundry, with his son Frank and daughter Dolly.

The front seat passenger in this chauffeur-driven car was Alderman Joseph Malins JP. He was Grand Chief Templar of the International Order of Good Templars. He was visiting Ilfracombe on Empire Day 1913. At the age of seventy he was retiring after forty-four years and, according to the *Ilfracombe Chronicle*, 'taking a farewell of every District in the Country'.

This photograph was taken in the stable yard of the Queen's Hotel, January 1926. It shows the last of the local horse-drawn post office vans about to be superseded by a motor vehicle.

In Bengey and Sons' coal yard a delivery lorry is evidently taking over from the horse and cart.

A very early open-sided charabanc about to take the Ilfracombe Methodist Choir on an outing to Clovelly, May 1912.

J.C. Millman had set up business at 102 High Street by the 1880s. He combined this with a boarding house and dining and refreshment rooms, and by the 1920s was using this van for deliveries.

Another outing to Clovelly, June 1911.

The staff of Ilfracombe station in the 1920s.

One of W.H. Gubb and Sons' Lucky Violet charabancs outside the Wesleyan church with a full load of passengers.

Colwill's No. 1 bus outside Ilfracombe station, *c.* 1920.

Copp, like Colwill, had moved on from horse-drawn coaches to charabancs by the 1920s. Here is one of his Silver Cars about to leave for Lynton in June, 1921.

SECTION SEVEN

SHIPS, BOATS AND LIFEBOATS

This engraving shows the *Great Britain* encountering rough weather off the coast of north Devon.

As large waves pound the pier, the *Spray* of Newport makes for Ilfracombe harbour.

As early as 1815 Ilfracombe's customs officer, Thomas Rodd, suggested that a lifeboat should be available in the harbour. Seven years later a writer noted that 'three large skiffs cruise here in the winter season for the express purpose of assisting vessels in distress'. No details of later lifeboats are available until the *Broadwater*, seen here in front of the Royal Britannia Hotel, began service in 1866 as an RNLI boat.

The *Grace Woodbury*, stationed at Woolacombe by the RNLI in 1871 as a subsidiary to the Ilfracombe boat. However, because of the difficulty of launching her from the beach, using horses, she only went out on rescue twice in twenty-nine years, and was then withdrawn. When Prince Frederick William of Prussia (the future Kaiser Wilhelm II) was staying at the Ilfracombe Hotel in 1878, he visited Woolacombe to watch the *Grace Woodbury*'s quarterly exercise.

This scene of the crew manhandling the lifeboat ashore in the harbour was sold as a postcard, 'The Return of the Lifeboat', in 1907.

A well-attended lifeboat service near the lifeboat house, 1913.

In the days when West Country sailing ketches delivered cargoes of many kinds around the coast, they were frequently beached to be unloaded into horse-drawn carts. Here coal is being delivered at Hele, less than a mile east of Ilfracombe.

These ketches are unloading in Ilfracombe harbour; the long-lived *Kate* is among them.

The inner harbour, 1880s. The ketch on the left has been identified as the *Jane*, built at Runcorn in 1800; astern is *Honor*, built in Jersey. The fore and aft schooner with sails drying is *Albion*.

This photograph dates from the days when the Quay, lined with fishing boats, was not walled.

The *Rowena*, 1925. Crew members were John Irwin ('Roscoe'), George Irwin ('Nobby'), Cyril Irwin and Jim Braund. The men in the gig were E. Ley and Tom Souch.

Tom Rudd mending his nets in the harbour at low tide.

P. and A. Campbell's splendid paddle steamer *Waverley* coming in to pick up excursion passengers at the pier, 1890s. She had been known as 'the Clipper of the Clyde', but on coming south to Bristol she was said to have earned the title of 'the Greyhound of the Bristol Channel'.

In the late nineteenth century and early twentieth century, as many as six paddle steamers could lie side by side at the pier, and passengers sometimes had to make their way across several ships to re-embark.

The paddle steamer *Brighton*, described by the Campbell brothers as a 'powerful sea-going saloon steamer'.

Passengers aboard PS *Cambria* in June 1913, with a Scotsman among them as though to emphasize the Scottish ownership of the steamer. The *Cambria*, like most of the Campbell fleet, made trips to Clovelly, Lundy, Lynmouth, Cardiff, Swansea, Clevedon and Bristol.

The Campbell fleet of paddle steamers was requisitioned for service in both world wars. Here *Glen Rosa, Harlequin, Monarchy* and *Waverley*, converted to minesweepers, await reconversion to peacetime work in January 1919.

The imposing PS *Bristol Queen* was apparently ordered by Campbell's from Charles Hill of Bristol the moment the Second World War ended. She has been described as 'representing the ultimate in paddler design'. She sailed majestically down the coasts of Somerset and Devon in September 1946 on her maiden voyage, carrying 600 passengers, and her approach to Ilfracombe was greeted by the jubilant firing of rockets.

By the later years of the twentieth century it was no longer necessary for the crew to manhandle the lifeboat on to its cradle in the inner harbour, as in 1907 – and with the bigger modern boat it would have been hardly possible. This is the *Robert and Phemia Brown*.

The *Snowflake*, for many years a familiar sight in Ilfracombe harbour. She was a 'Clyde Puffer', built in 1893. The Irwin family of Combe Martin bought her in 1898, and sailed her for forty-three years. She carried coal and general cargo in winter, but in summer, her hold washed and painted white, she carried strawberries and early potatoes to Swansea and other places.

Lundy's retiring supply ship, *Lundy Gannet*, passing her replacement, *Polar Bear*, in the outer harbour in 1976, bound for Cardiff after twenty years in service. *Polar Bear* served the island for fourteen years, but for much of that time was based at Bideford.

SECTION EIGHT

BEACHES AND COAST

Looking east from the Capstone, Lantern Hill is dwarfed by the mass of Hillsborough.

Rapparee beach in the lee of Hillsborough. In 1878, while he was staying at the Ilfracombe Hotel, Crown Prince Frederick Wilhelm, later Kaiser Wilhelm II, is said to have had a fight with a young boatman called Alfred Price, whose father owned bathing huts on this beach, because he wouldn't stop throwing stones at the huts. The incident was hushed up at the time. When the First World War broke out, Price became something of a local hero when a set of doggerel verses was published in Ilfracombe describing the fight. The writer was Will Coates, who wrote the words of the song 'Coachman Sam'.

Looking down on Rapparee beach and the harbour mouth, with a paddle steamer at the pier.

Rapparee Pleasure Gardens, 1930s.

Hardly recognizable today, this is Wildersmouth beach as it looked before any part of the area between the Capstone and the High Street had been developed.

Wildersmouth again, several decades later. The fact that the freighter is sailing so close inshore indicates the depth of water north of the Capstone.

In this photograph of Wildersmouth in Edwardian days the Ilfracombe Hotel swimming baths may be seen in the distance, with the Granville Hotel, opened in 1891, on the clifftop beyond.

Well-dressed and decorous Edwardians stroll along Capstone Parade, cut some sixty years earlier.

These three – two men and a woman – are said to be at the Tunnels, and their dress suggests that the photograph was taken *c.* 1870. Yet at that time the sexes were strictly segregated there.

Looking west along the coast, with the Ladies' bathing beach immediately below. The writer who noted the segregation arrangements in 1840 said that 'machines and bathing women are in attendance'. At the time this photograph was taken, showing bathing machines on the beach, the wall along the rocks built to enclose a safe pool for bathing had not yet been built.

A later photograph, showing the tidal pool.

This postcard captioned 'Mixed Bathing at Ilfracombe' was on sale a year or two after segregation ended in 1905.

SECTION NINE

PLACES NEARBY

The coast eastwards of Watermouth Castle, with Great Hangman in the distance.

Despite its appearance, Watermouth Castle is 'sham antique', having been built in the 1820s. It was owned by the Bassett family during the nineteenth century.

Looking down on Hele beach from Hillsborough.

The coast road east of Ilfracombe, along which Sam Colwill's four-horse excursion coach 'Benita' regularly travelled to Lynton every summer from 1875 until shortly before the First World War.

An engraving of Hele Valley as it once was. A writer in the 1850s saw Hele 'embosomed in gardens and orchards and half-hidden by tall and shaggy elms'.

The corn mill at Hele Bay, said to date from the sixteenth century. It has been restored to full working order, and is now a tourist attraction where visitors can buy freshly ground wholemeal flour.

The old thatched cottage at Lee, to the west of Ilfracombe, as it was in 1904.

Bull Point lighthouse, built in 1879 at a cost of £7,000, as it was before the landslide of September 1972. A new lighthouse was built in 1974.

A nineteenth-century engraving of Lee Bay.

Lee Bay, 1885. The man leaning against the wall was the coastguard.

Mortehoe, *c.* 1880. Lifesaving rocket apparatus was kept in the small building in the right foreground.

St Mary's church, Mortehoe, *c.* 1900.

Woolacombe beach with bathing machines in Edwardian days.

Like many places on the Devon coasts, Woolacombe had a limekiln, just seen here on the right. Limestone and culm for burning it were brought in by sea and unloaded on the beach.

Women with donkeys and a pony trap above Barricane beach, Woolacombe, *c.* 1910.

Barricane beach, at a time when donkey rides were for adults rather than children.

Woolacombe beach in winter, with bathing machines laid up on the sandy ground above the limekiln.

Woolacombe beach, showing the recently built Woolacombe Bay Hotel, originally known as Shakespeare's Hotel, *c.* 1890.

A closer view of the Woolacombe Bay Hotel, so successful that in 1897 it was enlarged.

SECTION TEN

ILFRACOMBE MUSEUM AND ITS FIRST CURATOR

A newcomer who settled in Ilfracombe in 1930 was evidently surprised to find that the town had neither a public library nor a museum. Within the next few years he brought about the establishment of both.

He was Mervyn Grove Palmer, a Fellow of both the Royal Geographical Society and the Royal Entomological Society, as well as a member of the British Ornithological Union. Educated at Alleyn's School, he trained as an analytical chemist and worked for a time in industry, but in 1904, when he was about twenty-three, he set off for Central America. As a collecting naturalist for the British and other museums, he travelled around Nicaragua, Columbia and Ecuador for six years. He discovered some fifty species new to science, including mammals, birds, reptiles and fish, a fact acknowledged by the inclusion of *palmeri* in their nomenclature. He specialized in zoology but also studied archaeology and ethnography. He travelled on horseback from Columbia to Ecuador, and on foot in the High Andes. His recollections of these early experiences, *Through Unknown Nicaragua*, were published in 1945.

In 1910 he began to work for the Singer Sewing Machine Company in Columbia, and later joined a firm of papermakers, Charles Morgan and Co. A tireless traveller, he claimed to have visited every country in South America except Paraguay, as well as the United States, Canada and the West Indies, and several European countries.

Having retired – apparently reluctantly – at the age of forty-nine, and settled in Ilfracombe, he busied himself with the formation of a museum committee, which held its first meeting in February 1931. Interest in the project grew rapidly, but one difficulty was the choice of a suitable building. The Ilfracombe Urban District Council, which had taken a lease of the west wing of the Ilfracombe Hotel for use as offices, made the offer of the hotel's former laundry building. When this had been suitably converted Mervyn

Palmer, who had naturally enough been appointed curator, was able to begin the preparation of exhibits. He decided on an experimental one-day opening on 1 August 1932, with free admission. The fact that 1,231 people visited the museum on that day – a figure not to be exceeded until 13 August 1974 – indicates the immense interest that had been generated.

Since then the museum has increased considerably in size, interest and diversity, and especially since 1983, when Mrs Joy Slocombe was appointed curator, has developed into one of the liveliest and most visited small museums in the west of England, with a warm and welcoming atmosphere. Attendance figures passed the two million mark several years ago. An eleven-year-old visitor at Easter 1993, Katherine Rawson from Birmingham, was so taken with the museum that she wrote an essay about it which came second out of nearly 18,000 entries in a competition organized by the BBC's 'Blue Peter' in association with English Heritage.

A new wing was opened in 1982. There are now seven rooms displaying over 20,000 items gathered by curators and trustees over sixty years. They include exhibits recalling Ilfracombe's maritime past and local history, militaria and costumes, birds, butterflies and moths, archaeological finds, maps and paintings and much else, including a Victorian kitchen and a brass-rubbing centre. The remarkable collection of several thousand photographs has provided the material for this book.

The museum, a registered charity, is managed by a board of Trustees, and its only source of income is the modest admission fee; school parties who book in advance are not charged.

Mervyn Palmer preparing for his first expedition to Nicaragua, 1904.

Ilfracombe Museum, by Sally Hills.

ACKNOWLEDGEMENTS

I would like to offer grateful thanks to the following:

The Trustees of Ilfracombe Museum for permission to reproduce the photographs, all from the museum's extensive collection, which make up this book; Mrs Joy Slocombe, curator of the museum, for her kindness and helpfulness; her staff, and in particular Miss Edna Baker, whose special care is the photographic collection.